The Daily Finnish Challe

Learn 10 Finnish Words a Day for 7 Weeks

Introduction

🎊 Welcome to "Learn 10 Finnish Words a Day for 7 Weeks"! This book is designed to provide an engaging and effective learning experience for children 🌱 and beginners 🌱 who are eager to discover the beauty of the Finnish language 🏴. With its carefully curated selection of words and interactive approach 👍, this book aims to make language learning a fun 🎈 and enjoyable journey.

Learning a new language can be both exciting 🌟 and challenging 🌑, but fear not! We have crafted this book with your learning needs in mind. Each day, you will encounter a set of ten Finnish words 🏴 that are carefully chosen to be useful and practical in everyday situations. These words cover various themes ⊕, allowing you to expand your vocabulary and gain confidence in your language skills.

To facilitate your learning process, we have provided corresponding English 🏴 words alongside the Finnish words, allowing you to establish meaningful connections 🔗 between the two languages. By actively engaging in writing down (4x) ✏️ the correct Finnish words, you will reinforce your memory and develop a solid foundation in the language. Embrace the joy of discovery 🎉 as you unlock new words each day, steadily building your language skills step by step.

This book is meant to be your companion 📔 throughout the course of seven weeks, providing you with a structured learning experience. Each week is carefully planned to introduce new vocabulary ◼ while reinforcing previously learned words, allowing you to review and consolidate your knowledge. Make sure to allocate a few minutes ⬢ each day to engage with the exercises and activities provided. Consistency is key 🔑, and your dedication will yield rewarding results 🏆.

Whether you are a young language enthusiast 🏆 or a curious beginner, this book is designed to cater to your needs. The vibrant illustrations 🎨 and interactive exercises are intended to spark your imagination 💭 and keep you engaged. Remember, learning a language should be an enjoyable experience ⚫, and we hope this book will ignite your passion for Finnish.

As you embark on this language learning adventure 🚀, we encourage you to embrace the challenge, celebrate your progress 🎊, and have fun along the way. Learning 10 Finnish words a day is an achievable goal ▦, and with perseverance and dedication, you will unlock the doors ▮ to a new world of communication and understanding ⚫.

Happy learning! ◉▪🎉

Attention: The provided English pronunciations of the Finnish words are approximations. The actual pronunciation may vary depending on regional accents and dialects in Finland. Furthermore, some Finnish sounds cannot be precisely reproduced in English, meaning that the pronunciations can slightly deviate from the original Finnish sounds.

Table of Contents

Week 1

Day 1: Numbers

One	Yksi [UUK-see]
Two	Kaksi [KAHK-see]
Three	Kolme [KOHL-meh]
Four	Neljä [NEL-yah]
Five	Viisi [VEE-see]
Six	Kuusi [KOO-see]
Seven	Seitsemän [SAYT-seh-mahn]
Eight	Kahdeksan [KAHD-ehk-sahn]
Nine	Yhdeksän [UUD-ehk-sahn]
Ten	Kymmenen [KUUM-meh-nen]

Write the right words down twice on the next page

Six	....	....
Two	....	....
Eight	....	....
Four	....	....
Five	....	....
Eight	....	....
Seven	....	....
Three	....	....
Nine	....	....
Ten	....	....
One	....	....
Two	....	....
Ten	....	....
Four	....	....
Five	....	....
Six	....	....
Seven	....	....
Three	....	....
Nine	....	....
One	....	....

Week 1

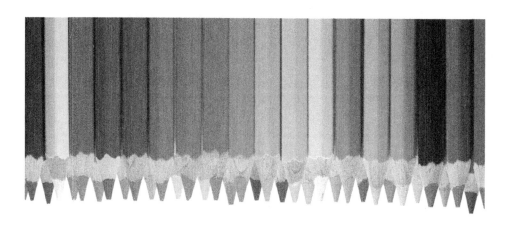

Day 2: Colors

Red	Punainen [POO-nigh-nen]
Blue	Sininen [SEE-nee-nen]
Yellow	Keltainen [KEL-tie-nen]
Green	Vihreä [VEE-hray-ah]
Orange	Oranssi [O-ran-ssi]
Purple	Violetti [VEE-oh-let-ti]
Pink	Vaaleanpunainen [VAH-leh-an-poo-nigh-nen]
Black	Musta [MOOS-tah]
White	Valkoinen [VAL-koy-nen]
Gray	Harmaa [HAR-mah]

Write the right words down twice on the next page

Red	....	....
Purple	....	....
White	....	....
Gray	....	....
Orange	....	....
Purple	....	....
Blue	....	....
Black	....	....
White	....	....
Gray	....	....
Pink	....	....
Blue	....	....
Yellow	....	....
Green	....	....
Orange	....	....
Pink	....	....
Red	....	....
Black	....	....
Yellow	....	....
Green	....	....

Week 1

Day 3: Family

Mother	Äiti [EYE-ti]
Father	Isä [EE-sa]
Brother	Veljekset [VEL-yek-set]
Sister	Siskot [SIS-kot]
Son	Poika [POY-kah]
Daughter	Tyttö [TUT-tö]
Grandfather	Isoisä [EE-soy-sa]
Grandmother	Isoäiti [EE-soy-ti]
Uncle	Setä [SE-ta]
Aunt	Täti [TA-ti]

Write the right words down twice on the next page

Aunt	....	....
Father	....	....
Mother	....	....
Uncle	....	....
Brother	....	....
Sister	....	....
Son	....	....
Daughter	....	....
Grandfather	....	....
Sister	....	....
Aunt	....	....
Grandmother	....	....
Uncle	....	....
Son	....	....
Grandmother	....	....
Father	....	....
Brother	....	....
Daughter	....	....
Grandfather	....	....
Mother	....	....

Week 1

Day 4: Food

Bread	Leipä [LAY-pah]
Rice	Riisi [REE-see]
Meat	Liha [LEE-hah]
Vegetables	Vihannekset [VEE-hahn-nek-set]
Fruit	Hedelmät [HEH-del-mat]
Milk	Maito [MIGH-toh]
Cheese	Juusto [YOO-sto]
Eggs	Munat [MOO-nat]
Soup	Keitto [KAYT-toh]
Dessert	Jälkiruoka [YAL-kee-ruoh-kah]

Write the right words down twice on the next page

Cheese	....	....
Meat	....	....
Dessert	....	....
Vegetables	....	....
Fruit	....	....
Milk	....	....
Vegetables	....	....
Eggs	....	....
Soup	....	....
Dessert	....	....
Bread	....	....
Rice	....	....
Meat	....	....
Fruit	....	....
Milk	....	....
Cheese	....	....
Bread	....	....
Eggs	....	....
Soup	....	....
Rice	....	....

Week 1

Day 5: Animals

Dog	Koira [KOY-rah]
Cat	Kissa [KIS-sah]
Lion	Leijona [LAY-yoh-nah]
Sheep	Lammas [LAM-mas]
Pig	Sika [SEE-kah]
Monkey	Apina [AH-pee-nah]
Tiger	Tiikeri [TEE-keh-ree]
Bear	Karhu [KAR-hu]
Horse	Hevonen [HEH-voh-nen]
Bird	Lintu [LEEN-tu]

Write the right words down twice on the next page

Monkey	....	....
Cat	....	....
Bird	....	....
Lion	....	....
Sheep	....	....
Pig	....	....
Monkey	....	....
Tiger	....	....
Bear	....	....
Horse	....	....
Bird	....	....
Dog	....	....
Cat	....	....
Lion	....	....
Sheep	....	....
Pig	....	....
Horse	....	....
Tiger	....	....
Bear	....	....
Dog	....	....

Week 1

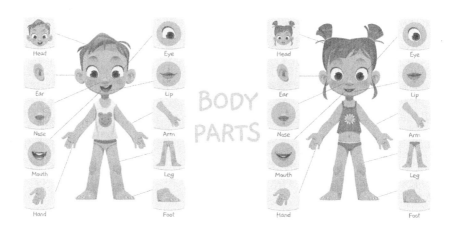

Day 6: Body

Head	Pää [PAH]
Neck	Niska [NEES-kah]
Belly	Vatsa [VAT-sah]
Shoulder	Olkapää [OL-kah-PAH]
Knee	Polvi [POL-vee]
Back	Selkä [SEL-kah]
Arms	Kädet [KAH-det]
Hands	Aseet [AH-seh-et]
Legs	Jalat [YAH-lat]
Feet	Jalat [YAH-lat]

Write the right words down twice on the next page

Shoulder	....	....
Back	....	....
Feet	....	....
Belly	....	....
Hands	....	....
Shoulder	....	....
Knee	....	....
Back	....	....
Arms	....	....
Hands	....	....
Neck	....	....
Feet	....	....
Head	....	....
Neck	....	....
Belly	....	....
Knee	....	....
Legs	....	....
Arms	....	....
Head	....	....
Legs	....	....

Week 1

Day 7: Weather

Sun	Aurinko [OW-rin-ko]
Rain	Sade [SAH-deh]
Cloud	Pilvi [PIL-vee]
Wind	Tuuli [TOO-lee]
Snow	Lumi [LOO-mee]
Thunder	Ukkonen [OOK-koh-nen]
Lightning	Salama [SAH-lah-mah]
Storm	Myrsky [MUR-sky]
Fog	Sumu [SOO-moo]
Rainbow	Sateenkaari [SAH-teen-KAH-ree]

Write the right words down twice on the next page

Storm	....	....
Rain	....	....
Fog	....	....
Snow	....	....
Cloud	....	....
Wind	....	....
Snow	....	....
Thunder	....	....
Rain	....	....
Lightning	....	....
Storm	....	....
Fog	....	....
Rainbow	....	....
Sun	....	....
Cloud	....	....
Wind	....	....
Thunder	....	....
Lightning	....	....
Rainbow	....	....
Sun	....	....

Week 2

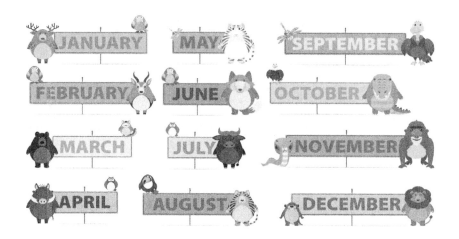

Day 8: Months

January	Tammikuu [TAM-mee-koo]
February	Helmikuu [HEL-mee-koo]
March	Maaliskuu [MAH-lee-skoo]
April	Huhtikuu [HUH-ti-koo]
May	Toukokuu [TOU-ko-koo]
June	Kesäkuu [KEH-sa-koo]
July	Heinäkuu [HAY-na-koo]
August	Elokuu [E-lo-koo]
September	Syyskuu [SYYS-koo]
October	Lokakuu [LO-ka-koo]

Write the right words down twice on the next page

October	....	....
February	....	....
August	....	....
October	....	....
April	....	....
May	....	....
June	....	....
August	....	....
March	....	....
September	....	....
May	....	....
January	....	....
July	....	....
March	....	....
April	....	....
June	....	....
January	....	....
July	....	....
February	....	....
September	....	....

Week 2

Day 9: School

Teacher	Opettaja [O-peh-TAH-ja]
Student	Opiskelija [O-pis-KE-li-ja]
Classroom	Luokkahuone [LU-oh-kka-HUO-ne]
Book	Kirja [KEER-ja]
Pen	Kynä [KU-na]
Pencil	Lyijykynä [LU-ee-yu-KU-na]
Desk	Pöytä [POY-ta]
Chair	Tuoli [TUO-lee]
Homework	Kotitehtävä [KO-ti-TEH-ta-va]
Exam	Koe [KOH-eh]

Write the right words down twice on the next page

Chair	....	....
Homework	....	....
Teacher	....	....
Student	....	....
Classroom	....	....
Exam	....	....
Pen	....	....
Pencil	....	....
Desk	....	....
Classroom	....	....
Homework	....	....
Exam	....	....
Teacher	....	....
Student	....	....
Desk	....	....
Book	....	....
Pen	....	....
Pencil	....	....
Chair	....	....
Book	....	....

Week 2

Day 10: Transportation

Car	Auto [OW-to]
Bus	Bussi [BOO-ssi]
Train	Juna [YOU-nah]
Bicycle	Polkupyörä [POL-ku-PYU-ra]
Motorcycle	Moottoripyörä [MO-tori-PYU-ra]
Boat	Vene [VEH-neh]
Airplane	Lentokone [LEN-to-KO-ne]
Helicopter	Helikopteri [HE-lik-OP-te-ri]
Truck	Kuorma-auto [KUOR-ma-OW-to]
Metro	Metro [MET-ro]

Write the right words down twice on the next page

Airplane	....	....
Bus	....	....
Train	....	....
Metro	....	....
Truck	....	....
Motorcycle	....	....
Boat	....	....
Airplane	....	....
Helicopter	....	....
Truck	....	....
Metro	....	....
Car	....	....
Bus	....	....
Train	....	....
Bicycle	....	....
Helicopter	....	....
Motorcycle	....	....
Boat	....	....
Bicycle	....	....
Car	....	....

Week 2

Day 11: Clothing

Shirt	Paita [PIE-tah]
Pants	Housut [HOO-sut]
Dress	Mekko [MEK-ko]
Skirt	Hame [HAH-meh]
Jacket	Takki [TAK-kee]
Shoes	Kengät [KEN-gat]
Socks	Sukat [SOO-kat]
Hat	Hattu [HAT-too]
Gloves	Hanskat [HAN-skah]
Scarf	Kaulahuivi [KAU-lah-HOO-vee]

Write the right words down twice on the next page

Socks	....	....
Pants	....	....
Dress	....	....
Jacket	....	....
Skirt	....	....
Scarf	....	....
Shoes	....	....
Socks	....	....
Hat	....	....
Gloves	....	....
Scarf	....	....
Shirt	....	....
Pants	....	....
Dress	....	....
Skirt	....	....
Jacket	....	....
Shoes	....	....
Gloves	....	....
Hat	....	....
Shirt	....	....

Week 2

Day 12: Emotions

Happy	Iloinen [IL-oy-nen]
Sad	Surullinen [SOO-roo-lee-nen]
Angry	Vihainen [VEE-hy-nen]
Excited	Innoissaan [IN-nois-saan]
Surprised	Yllättynyt [YL-lat-ty-nut]
Scared	Pelokas [PE-lo-kas]
Nervous	Hermostunut [HER-mos-tu-nut]
Bored	Tylsistynyt [TUL-sis-ty-nut]
Confused	Ymmällään [YM-mal-lan]
Calm	Rauhallinen [RAU-hal-linen]

Write the right words down twice on the next page

Confused ....

Happy ....

Calm ....

Surprised ....

Sad ....

Angry ....

Excited ....

Nervous ....

Scared ....

Nervous ....

Bored ....

Scared ....

Calm ....

Happy ....

Sad ....

Bored ....

Angry ....

Excited ....

Surprised ....

Confused ....

Week 2

Day 13: Hobbies

Reading	Lukeminen [LOO-keh-mi-nen]
Painting	Maalaaminen [MAA-laa-mi-nen]
Singing	Laulaminen [LAU-la-mi-nen]
Dancing	Tanssiminen [TAN-ssi-mi-nen]
Cooking	Ruuanlaitto [ROO-an-LIGH-to]
Photography	Valokuvaus [VAL-o-KOO-vaus]
Sleeping	Nukkuminen [NOOK-koo-mi-nen]
Writing	Kirjoittaminen [KEER-oy-ta-mi-nen]
Gardening	Puutarhanhoito [POO-tar-HAN-hoy-to]
Sports	Urheilu [UR-hay-loo]

Write the right words down twice on the next page

Gardening ....

Painting ....

Photography ....

Painting ....

Dancing ....

Cooking ....

Photography ....

Sports ....

Writing ....

Gardening ....

Sports ....

Reading ....

Sleeping ....

Singing ....

Dancing ....

Cooking ....

Singing ....

Sleeping ....

Writing ....

Reading ....

Week 2

Day 14: Sports

Football   Jalkapallo [YAL-ka-PAL-lo]

Basketball   Koripallo [KO-ri-PAL-lo]

Tennis   Tennis [TEN-nis]

Swimming   Uinti [OO-in-ti]

Volleyball   Lentopallo [LEN-to-PAL-lo]

Golf   Golf [GOLF]

Cycling   Pyöräily [PYO-ra-ily]

Running   Juokseminen [YOO-kse-mi-nen]

Fitness   Kuntoilu [KUN-toy-loo]

Martial arts   Kamppailulajit [KAM-pai-lu-LA-yit]

Write the right words down twice on the next page

Swimming	....	....
Football	....	....
Fitness	....	....
Basketball	....	....
Golf	....	....
Swimming	....	....
Volleyball	....	....
Golf	....	....
Running	....	....
Cycling	....	....
Running	....	....
Fitness	....	....
Martial arts	....	....
Football	....	....
Basketball	....	....
Tennis	....	....
Martial arts	....	....
Volleyball	....	....
Cycling	....	....
Tennis	....	....

Week 3

Day 15: Nature

Tree	Puu [POO]
Flower	Kukka [KOOK-kah]
River	Joki [YO-kee]
Mountain	Vuori [VOO-ri]
Lake	Järvi [YAR-vee]
Beach	Ranta [RAN-tah]
Forest	Metsä [MET-sa]
Grass	Ruoho [ROO-ho]
Star	Tähti [TAH-tee]
Cloud	Pilvi [PIL-vee]

Write the right words down twice on the next page

Grass	....	....
Beach	....	....
Mountain	....	....
Cloud	....	....
Flower	....	....
River	....	....
Mountain	....	....
Lake	....	....
Beach	....	....
Forest	....	....
Grass	....	....
Star	....	....
Forest	....	....
Cloud	....	....
Tree	....	....
Flower	....	....
River	....	....
Star	....	....
Lake	....	....
Tree	....	....

Week 3

Day 16: Days of the Week

Monday	Maanantai [MAA-nan-tai]
Tuesday	Tiistai [TEES-tai]
Wednesday	Keskiviikko [KES-kee-VIK-ko]
Thursday	Torstai [TOR-stai]
Friday	Perjantai [PER-yan-tai]
Saturday	Lauantai [LAU-an-tai]
Sunday	Sunnuntai [SUN-nun-tai]
Yesterday	Eilen [EYE-len]
Tomorrow	Huomenna [HOO-oh-men-na]
Today	Tänään [TAN-an]

Write the right words down twice on the next page

Sunday	....	....
Tuesday	....	....
Saturday	....	....
Today	....	....
Wednesday	....	....
Tomorrow	....	....
Friday	....	....
Saturday	....	....
Yesterday	....	....
Tomorrow	....	....
Today	....	....
Monday	....	....
Thursday	....	....
Wednesday	....	....
Thursday	....	....
Friday	....	....
Monday	....	....
Sunday	....	....
Yesterday	....	....
Tuesday	....	....

Week 3

Day 17: Music

Song	Laulu [LAU-lu]
Melody	Melodia [ME-lo-dee-a]
Rhythm	Rytmi [RUT-mi]
Instrument	Soitin [SOY-tin]
Singing	Laulaminen [LAU-la-mi-nen]
Band	Bändi [BAND-dee]
Concert	Konsertti [KON-ser-tti]
Piano	Piano [PEE-a-no]
Guitar	Kitara [KEE-ta-ra]
Sound	Ääni [A-ni]

Write the right words down twice on the next page

Concert	....	....
Melody	....	....
Rhythm	....	....
Sound	....	....
Guitar	....	....
Piano	....	....
Instrument	....	....
Singing	....	....
Band	....	....
Piano	....	....
Guitar	....	....
Sound	....	....
Song	....	....
Rhythm	....	....
Instrument	....	....
Singing	....	....
Band	....	....
Concert	....	....
Song	....	....
Melody	....	....

Week 3

Day 18: Jobs

Teacher	Opettaja [O-peh-TAH-ja]
Doctor	Lääkäri [LAY-ka-ri]
Engineer	Insinööri [IN-si-NOO-ri]
Chef	Kokki [KOK-kee]
Police officer	Poliisi [PO-lee-see]
Firefighter	Palomies [PA-lo-mies]
Nurse	Sairaanhoitaja [SAI-ran-HOI-ta-ja]
Pilot	Pilotti [PEE-lot-tee]
Lawyer	Asianajaja [AH-see-an-AH-ya-ya]
Artist	Taiteilija [TAI-te-lee-ja]

Write the right words down twice on the next page

Lawyer	....	....
Teacher	....	....
Chef	....	....
Doctor	....	....
Engineer	....	....
Chef	....	....
Police officer	....	....
Pilot	....	....
Nurse	....	....
Doctor	....	....
Artist	....	....
Teacher	....	....
Pilot	....	....
Engineer	....	....
Artist	....	....
Police officer	....	....
Firefighter	....	....
Nurse	....	....
Lawyer	....	....
Firefighter	....	....

Week 3

Day 19: Fruits

Apple	Omena [O-men-a]
Banana	Banaani [BA-naa-ni]
Orange	Appelsiini [AP-pel-SEEN-i]
Strawberry	Mansikka [MAN-sik-ka]
Grapes	Viinirypäleet [VEE-nir-YPA-leet]
Watermelon	Vesimeloni [VES-i-ME-lo-ni]
Pineapple	Ananas [AH-na-nas]
Mango	Mango [MANG-o]
Kiwi	Kiivi [KEE-vee]
Peach	Persikka [PER-sik-ka]

Write the right words down twice on the next page

Orange	....	....
Apple	....	....
Banana	....	....
Orange	....	....
Mango	....	....
Grapes	....	....
Kiwi	....	....
Pineapple	....	....
Mango	....	....
Peach	....	....
Apple	....	....
Banana	....	....
Strawberry	....	....
Grapes	....	....
Watermelon	....	....
Pineapple	....	....
Kiwi	....	....
Strawberry	....	....
Peach	....	....
Watermelon	....	....

Week 3

Day 20: Vegetables

Carrot	Porkkana [POR-kka-na]
Tomato	Tomaatti [TO-maa-tti]
Potato	Peruna [PE-ru-na]
Onion	Sipuli [SI-pu-li]
Cucumber	Kurkku [KUR-kku]
Broccoli	Broccoli [BROK-ko-lee]
Spinach	Pinaatti [PIN-aa-tti]
Corn	Maissi [MAIS-see]
Cabbage	Kaalikasvi [KAA-li-KAS-vee]
Mushroom	Sieni [SEE-eni]

Write the right words down twice on the next page

Corn	....	....
Tomato	....	....
Potato	....	....
Mushroom	....	....
Spinach	....	....
Onion	....	....
Broccoli	....	....
Spinach	....	....
Corn	....	....
Tomato	....	....
Mushroom	....	....
Carrot	....	....
Cucumber	....	....
Potato	....	....
Onion	....	....
Cucumber	....	....
Cabbage	....	....
Carrot	....	....
Cabbage	....	....
Broccoli	....	....

Week 3

Day 21: Tools

Hammer	Vasara [VA-sa-ra]
Screwdriver	Ruuvimeisseli [ROO-vi-MEIS-se-li]
Wrench	Pihdit [PEE-hit]
Pliers	Kiintoavain [KEEN-to-ava-in]
Saw	Saha [SA-ha]
Drill	Porakone [PO-ra-ko-ne]
Tape measure	Mittanauha [MIT-ta-NAU-ha]
Chisel	Taltta [TAL-tta]
Level	Lapio [LA-pio]
Paintbrush	Maalipensseli [MAAL-i-PEN-sse-li]

Write the right words down twice on the next page

Level ....

Screwdriver ....

Wrench ....

Paintbrush ....

Pliers ....

Drill ....

Chisel ....

Level ....

Paintbrush ....

Hammer ....

Screwdriver ....

Pliers ....

Saw ....

Drill ....

Tape measure ....

Hammer ....

Wrench ....

Saw ....

Chisel ....

Tape measure ....

Week 4

Day 22: Kitchen

Plate	Lautanen [LAU-ta-nen]
Fork	Haarukka [HAA-ruk-ka]
Knife	Veitsi [VEIT-si]
Spoon	Lusikka [LU-sik-ka]
Cup	Kuppi [KUP-pi]
Bowl	Kulho [KUL-ho]
Pan	Paistinpannu [PAIS-tin-PAN-nu]
Pot	Kattila [KAT-tila]
Cutting board	Leikkuulauta [LEIK-ku-LAU-ta]
Oven	Uuni [OO-ni]

Write the right words down twice on the next page

Plate ....

Oven ....

Fork ....

Bowl ....

Knife ....

Spoon ....

Cup ....

Cutting board ....

Knife ....

Fork ....

Bowl ....

Spoon ....

Pan ....

Pot ....

Cutting board ....

Oven ....

Pot ....

Plate ....

Cup ....

Pan ....

Week 4

Day 23: Instruments

Guitar	Kitara [KEE-ta-ra]
Piano	Piano [PEE-a-no]
Violin	Viulu [VEE-u-lu]
Flute	Huilu [HUI-lu]
Trumpet	Trumpetti [TRUM-pet-ti]
Drum	Rumpu [RUM-pu]
Saxophone	Saksofoni [SAK-so-fo-ni]
Cello	Sello [SEL-lo]
Clarinet	Klarinetti [KLAR-in-et-ti]
Harp	Harppu [HAR-ppu]

Write the right words down twice on the next page

Flute	....	....
Piano	....	....
Trumpet	....	....
Violin	....	....
Cello	....	....
Trumpet	....	....
Drum	....	....
Saxophone	....	....
Cello	....	....
Clarinet	....	....
Violin	....	....
Saxophone	....	....
Harp	....	....
Guitar	....	....
Drum	....	....
Piano	....	....
Harp	....	....
Flute	....	....
Guitar	....	....
Clarinet	....	....

Week 4

Day 24: Buildings

House	Talo [TA-lo]
School	Koulu [KOU-lu]
Hospital	Sairaala [SAI-ra-ala]
Library	Kirjasto [KEER-yas-to]
Bank	Pankki [PANK-ki]
Restaurant	Ravintola [RA-vin-to-la]
Hotel	Hotelli [HO-tel-li]
Museum	Museo [MU-se-o]
Church	Kirkko [KEER-kko]
Stadium	Stadion [STA-dion]

Write the right words down twice on the next page

Hospital	....	....
House	....	....
Museum	....	....
School	....	....
Stadium	....	....
Hospital	....	....
Church	....	....
Restaurant	....	....
Hotel	....	....
Museum	....	....
Church	....	....
House	....	....
School	....	....
Library	....	....
Bank	....	....
Restaurant	....	....
Hotel	....	....
Library	....	....
Bank	....	....
Stadium	....	....

Week 4

Day 25: Directions

Left	Vasen [VA-sen]
Right	Oikea [OI-kea]
Straight	Suoraan [SUO-raan]
Up	Ylös [YLOS]
Down	Alas [A-las]
North	Pohjoinen [POH-yoi-nen]
South	Etelä [E-te-la]
East	Itä [IT-ta]
West	Länsi [LAN-si]
Stop	Pysäytys [PY-say-tys]

Write the right words down twice on the next page

Straight	....	....
Left	....	....
South	....	....
Straight	....	....
Up	....	....
Down	....	....
North	....	....
Stop	....	....
East	....	....
Stop	....	....
Left	....	....
Right	....	....
South	....	....
Right	....	....
North	....	....
West	....	....
Up	....	....
Down	....	....
East	....	....
West	....	....

Week 4

Day 26: Bedroom

Bed	Sänky [SANK-ky]
Pillow	Tyyny [TYYN-ny]
Blanket	Viltti [VILT-ti]
Wardrobe	Vaatekaappi [VA-te-KAAP-pi]
Nightstand	Yöpöytä [YO-poy-ta]
Lamp	Lamppu [LAM-ppu]
Alarm clock	Herätyskello [HE-rat-ys-KEL-lo]
Dresser	Pukeutumispöytä [PU-keu-tu-mis-POY-ta]
Hanger	Vaateripustin [VAA-te-RIP-us-tin]
Mirror	Peili [PEI-li]

Write the right words down twice on the next page

Hanger	....	....
Pillow	....	....
Dresser	....	....
Wardrobe	....	....
Mirror	....	....
Nightstand	....	....
Lamp	....	....
Alarm clock	....	....
Dresser	....	....
Blanket	....	....
Hanger	....	....
Mirror	....	....
Wardrobe	....	....
Nightstand	....	....
Bed	....	....
Blanket	....	....
Lamp	....	....
Bed	....	....
Alarm clock	....	....
Pillow	....	....

Week 4

Day 27: Countries

United States   Yhdysvallat [YHD-ys-VAL-lat]

United Kingdom   Yhdistynyt kuningaskunta [YHD-is-TY-nyt KU-nin-gas-KUN-ta]

Canada   Kanada [KA-na-da]

Australia   Australia [AUS-tra-li-a]

Germany   Saksa [SAK-sa]

France   Ranska [RAN-ska]

China   Kiina [KEE-na]

Japan   Japani [YA-pa-ni]

Brazil   Brasilia [BRA-si-li-a]

India   Intia [IN-ti-a]

Write the right words down twice on the next page

China ....

United States ....

India ....

Canada ....

Australia ....

Brazil ....

China ....

Japan ....

Brazil ....

India ....

United States ....

Germany ....

Canada ....

Australia ....

Japan ....

United Kingdom ....

Germany ....

France ....

United Kingdom ....

France ....

Week 4

Day 28: Travel

Airport	Lentokenttä [LEN-to-KEN-tta]
Passport	Passi [PAS-si]
Ticket	Lippu [LIP-pu]
Suitcase	Matkalaukku [MAT-ka-LAU-kku]
Hotel	Hotelli [HO-tel-li]
Sightseeing	Sightseeing [SIGHT-seeing] (English loanword)
Beach	Ranta [RAN-ta]
Adventure	Seikkailu [SEIK-kai-lu]
Map	Kartta [KART-ta]
Tourist	Turisti [TU-ris-ti]

Write the right words down twice on the next page

Airport	....	....
Adventure	....	....
Passport	....	....
Ticket	....	....
Suitcase	....	....
Hotel	....	....
Sightseeing	....	....
Beach	....	....
Adventure	....	....
Map	....	....
Tourist	....	....
Airport	....	....
Passport	....	....
Ticket	....	....
Suitcase	....	....
Hotel	....	....
Sightseeing	....	....
Beach	....	....
Map	....	....
Tourist	....	....

Week 5

Day 29: Health

Doctor	Lääkäri [LAY-ka-ri]
Hospital	Sairaala [SAI-ra-ala]
Medicine	Lääke [LAY-ke]
Nurse	Sairaanhoitaja [SAI-ran-HOI-ta-ja]
Pain	Kipu [KEE-pu]
Appointment	Vastaanotto [VAS-taan-OT-to]
Exercise	Liikunta [LEEK-un-ta]
Sleep	Uni [OO-ni]
Diet	Ruokavalio [ROO-ka-VA-li-o]
Vitamin	Vitamiini [VEE-ta-MEE-ni]

Write the right words down twice on the next page

Appointment	....	....
Vitamin	....	....
Hospital	....	....
Medicine	....	....
Nurse	....	....
Pain	....	....
Sleep	....	....
Hospital	....	....
Exercise	....	....
Nurse	....	....
Sleep	....	....
Diet	....	....
Vitamin	....	....
Doctor	....	....
Pain	....	....
Appointment	....	....
Exercise	....	....
Doctor	....	....
Medicine	....	....
Diet	....	....

Week 5

Day 30: Languages

English	Englanti [ENG-lan-ti]
Spanish	Espanja [ES-pan-ya]
Greek	Ranska [RAN-ska]
German	Saksa [SAK-sa]
Dutch	Hollanti [HOL-lan-ti]
Frisian	Friisi [FREE-si]
Russian	Venäjä [VE-nay-ya]
Portuguese	Portugali [POR-tu-GA-li]
Japanese	Japani [YA-pa-ni]
Italian	Italia [I-ta-li-a]

Write the right words down twice on the next page

German	....	....
Spanish	....	....
Portuguese	....	....
Greek	....	....
German	....	....
Dutch	....	....
Frisian	....	....
Russian	....	....
Italian	....	....
Russian	....	....
Japanese	....	....
Frisian	....	....
English	....	....
Italian	....	....
English	....	....
Spanish	....	....
Greek	....	....
Dutch	....	....
Portuguese	....	....
Japanese	....	....

Week 5

Day 31: Church

Priest	Pappi [PAP-pi]
Worship	Palvonta [PAL-von-ta]
Prayer	Rukous [RU-kous]
Bible	Raamattu [RAA-mat-tu]
Sermon	Saarna [SAAR-na]
Choir	Kuoro [KUO-ro]
Altar	Alttari [ALT-ta-ri]
Cross	Risti [RIS-ti]
Faith	Usko [US-ko]
Ceremony	Seremonia [se-re-MO-ni-a]

Write the right words down twice on the next page

Choir	....	....
Worship	....	....
Altar	....	....
Bible	....	....
Ceremony	....	....
Faith	....	....
Sermon	....	....
Choir	....	....
Altar	....	....
Cross	....	....
Faith	....	....
Ceremony	....	....
Cross	....	....
Priest	....	....
Worship	....	....
Prayer	....	....
Bible	....	....
Sermon	....	....
Priest	....	....
Prayer	....	....

Week 5

Day 32: Birds

Eagle	Kotka [KOT-ka]
Sparrow	Varpunen [VAR-pu-nen]
Owl	Pöllö [POL-lo]
Parrot	Papukaija [PA-pu-kai-ja]
Hummingbird	Kolibri [KO-li-bri]
Pigeon	Kyyhky [KYY-hky]
Flamingo	Flamingo [fla-MIN-go]
Swan	Joutsen [JOUT-sen]
Peacock	Riikinkukko [RII-kin-kuk-ko]
Duck	Ankka [ANK-ka]

Write the right words down twice on the next page

Duck	....	....
Eagle	....	....
Sparrow	....	....
Owl	....	....
Eagle	....	....
Swan	....	....
Sparrow	....	....
Flamingo	....	....
Hummingbird	....	....
Pigeon	....	....
Flamingo	....	....
Owl	....	....
Swan	....	....
Peacock	....	....
Duck	....	....
Parrot	....	....
Hummingbird	....	....
Pigeon	....	....
Parrot	....	....
Peacock	....	....

Week 5

Day 33: Science

Chemistry	Kemia [KE-mi-a]
Biology	Biologia [BIO-lo-gi-a]
Physics	Fysiikka [FYS-iik-ka]
Astronomy	Tähtitiede [TAHT-ti-tie-de]
Experiment	Koe [KO-e]
Laboratory	Laboratorio [la-BO-ra-to-ri-o]
Microscope	Mikroskooppi [MI-kro-skoo-ppi]
Hypothesis	Hypoteesi [hy-PO-te-esi]
Scientist	Tiedemies [TIE-de-mies]
Discovery	Löytö [LOY-to]

Write the right words down twice on the next page

Hypothesis	....	....
Biology	....	....
Experiment	....	....
Astronomy	....	....
Physics	....	....
Astronomy	....	....
Microscope	....	....
Scientist	....	....
Laboratory	....	....
Physics	....	....
Microscope	....	....
Hypothesis	....	....
Chemistry	....	....
Scientist	....	....
Discovery	....	....
Chemistry	....	....
Biology	....	....
Laboratory	....	....
Discovery	....	....
Experiment	....	....

Week 5

Day 34: Film

Actor	Näyttelijä [NAYT-te-li-ja]
Actress	Näyttelijätär [NAYT-te-li-ja-tar]
Director	Ohjaaja [OH-jaa-ja]
Script	Käsikirjoitus [KASI-kir-joi-tus]
Camera	Kamera [KA-mer-a]
Scene	Kohtaus [KOHT-aus]
Drama	Draama [DRAA-ma]
Comedy	Komedia [KO-me-di-a]
Action	Toiminta [TOI-min-ta]
Television	Televisio [te-LE-vi-sio]

Write the right words down twice on the next page

Actor	....	....
Camera	....	....
Action	....	....
Director	....	....
Script	....	....
Television	....	....
Camera	....	....
Scene	....	....
Drama	....	....
Comedy	....	....
Action	....	....
Television	....	....
Actor	....	....
Actress	....	....
Director	....	....
Scene	....	....
Actress	....	....
Drama	....	....
Comedy	....	....
Script	....	....

Week 5

Day 35: History

Ancient	Muinainen [MUI-nai-nen]
Civilization	Sivilisaatio [si-vi-li-SA-ti-o]
Emperor	Keisari [KEI-sa-ri]
Revolution	Vallankumous [VAL-lan-ku-mous]
War	Sota [SO-ta]
Kingdom	Kuningaskunta [KU-nin-gas-kun-ta]
Archaeology	Arkeologia [ar-ke-O-lo-gi-a]
Renaissance	Renessanssi [re-NES-sans-si]
Independence	Itsenäisyys [IT-se-NAI-syys]
Event	Tapahtuma [TA-pah-tu-ma]

Write the right words down twice on the next page

Kingdom	....	....
Event	....	....
Archaeology	....	....
Emperor	....	....
Renaissance	....	....
Independence	....	....
Revolution	....	....
War	....	....
Kingdom	....	....
Archaeology	....	....
Renaissance	....	....
Independence	....	....
Event	....	....
Ancient	....	....
Civilization	....	....
Emperor	....	....
Revolution	....	....
War	....	....
Ancient	....	....
Civilization	....	....

Week 6

Day 36: Drinks

Water	Vesi [VE-si]
Coffee	Kahvi [KAH-vi]
Tea	Tee [TE-e]
Juice	Mehu [ME-hu]
Soda	Soodavesi [SOO-da-ve-si]
Milk	Maito [MAI-to]
Wine	Viini [VEE-ni]
Beer	Olut [O-lut]
Cocktail	Cocktail [COCK-tail] (English pronunciation)
Lemonade	Limonadi [LI-mo-na-di]

Write the right words down twice on the next page

Soda	....	....
Cocktail	....	....
Tea	....	....
Juice	....	....
Wine	....	....
Soda	....	....
Milk	....	....
Wine	....	....
Beer	....	....
Cocktail	....	....
Lemonade	....	....
Water	....	....
Coffee	....	....
Water	....	....
Tea	....	....
Lemonade	....	....
Juice	....	....
Milk	....	....
Coffee	....	....
Beer	....	....

Week 6

Day 37: Business

Entrepreneur	Yrittäjä [YRIT-ta-ja]
Company	Yritys [YRI-tys]
Marketing	Markkinointi [MARK-ki-noin-ti]
Sales	Myynti [MYYN-ti]
Product	Tuote [TUO-te]
Customer	Asiakas [A-si-a-kas]
Finance	Rahoitus [RAH-oi-tus]
Strategy	Strategia [stra-TE-gi-a]
Profit	Voitto [VOIT-to]
Investment	Sijoitus [si-JOI-tus]

Write the right words down twice on the next page

Strategy	....	....
Company	....	....
Marketing	....	....
Sales	....	....
Product	....	....
Customer	....	....
Finance	....	....
Investment	....	....
Customer	....	....
Profit	....	....
Finance	....	....
Investment	....	....
Entrepreneur	....	....
Company	....	....
Marketing	....	....
Sales	....	....
Product	....	....
Profit	....	....
Entrepreneur	....	....
Strategy	....	....

Week 6

Day 38: Beach

Sand	Hiekka [HIEK-ka]
Waves	Aallot [AAL-lot]
Sunscreen	Auringonsuojavoide [AURIN-gon-su-o-ja-voi-de]
Swim	Uinti [UIN-ti]
Seashells	Simpukankuoria [SIM-pu-kan-KUO-ri-a]
Umbrella	Sateenvarjo [SA-te-en-VAR-jo]
Beach ball	Rantapallo [RAN-ta-pal-lo]
Sunbathing	Auringonotto [AURIN-gon-ot-to]
Surfing	Surffaaminen [SURF-fa-a-min-en]
Picnic	Piknik [PIK-nik] (English pronunciation)

Write the right words down twice on the next page

Beach ball	....	....
Sunbathing	....	....
Waves	....	....
Sunscreen	....	....
Picnic	....	....
Swim	....	....
Umbrella	....	....
Beach ball	....	....
Picnic	....	....
Sand	....	....
Sunscreen	....	....
Swim	....	....
Seashells	....	....
Surfing	....	....
Waves	....	....
Umbrella	....	....
Seashells	....	....
Sunbathing	....	....
Surfing	....	....
Sand	....	....

Week 6

Day 39: Hospital

Doctor	Lääkäri [LAY-ka-ri]
Nurse	Sairaanhoitaja [SAI-ran-HOI-ta-ja]
Patient	Potilas [PO-til-as]
Emergency	Hätätilanne [HA-ta-TI-lan-ne]
Surgery	Leikkaus [LEIK-kaus]
Appointment	Vastaanotto [VAS-taan-OT-to]
Stethoscope	Stetoskooppi [STE-to-SKOO-ppi]
X-ray	Röntgen [RONT-gen]
Medicine	Lääke [LAY-ke]
Recovery	Toipuminen [TOI-pu-min-en]

Write the right words down twice on the next page

Nurse	....	....
Doctor	....	....
Appointment	....	....
Stethoscope	....	....
Emergency	....	....
Recovery	....	....
Nurse	....	....
Patient	....	....
Emergency	....	....
Surgery	....	....
Appointment	....	....
Stethoscope	....	....
X-ray	....	....
Medicine	....	....
Recovery	....	....
Doctor	....	....
Surgery	....	....
Patient	....	....
X-ray	....	....
Medicine	....	....

Week 6

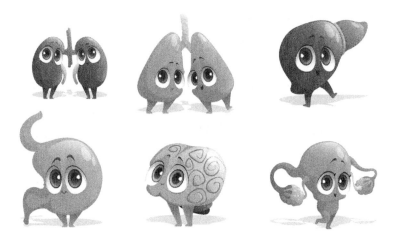

Day 40: Internal Body

Heart	Sydän [SY-dan]
Lungs	Keuhkot [KEUH-kot]
Stomach	Vatsa [VAT-sa]
Liver	Maksa [MAK-sa]
Kidneys	Munuaiset [MUN-uai-set]
Brain	Aivot [AI-vot]
Intestines	Suolisto [SUO-lis-to]
Bladder	Virtsarakko [VIR-tsa-rak-ko]
Bones	Luut [LU-ut]
Muscles	Lihas [LI-has]

Write the right words down twice on the next page

Kidneys	....	....
Stomach	....	....
Heart	....	....
Intestines	....	....
Brain	....	....
Lungs	....	....
Stomach	....	....
Liver	....	....
Muscles	....	....
Kidneys	....	....
Intestines	....	....
Bladder	....	....
Bones	....	....
Muscles	....	....
Heart	....	....
Lungs	....	....
Bones	....	....
Liver	....	....
Brain	....	....
Bladder	....	....

Week 6

Day 41: Internet

Website	Verkkosivusto [VERK-ko-sivus-to]
Email	Sähköposti [SAHK-o-pos-ti]
Social media	Sosiaalinen media [so-SIAA-li-nen ME-di-a]
Online shopping	Verkkokauppa [VERK-ko-kaup-pa]
Search engine	Hakukone [HA-ku-ko-ne]
Password	Salasana [SA-la-sa-na]
Wi-Fi	Wi-Fi [VEE-fee]
Download	Lataus [LA-taus]
Upload	Lähetys [LAHE-tys]
Browser	Selain [SE-lain]

Write the right words down twice on the next page

Browser ....

Website ....

Email ....

Social media ....

Wi-Fi ....

Search engine ....

Password ....

Wi-Fi ....

Download ....

Upload ....

Browser ....

Online shopping ....

Email ....

Social media ....

Online shopping ....

Password ....

Website ....

Download ....

Upload ....

Search engine ....

Week 6

Day 42: Shapes

Cirkel	Ympyrä [YMP-yra]
Square	Neliö [NE-li-o]
Rectangle	Suorakulmio [SUO-ra-kul-mio]
Triangle	Kolmio [KOL-mio]
Oval	Ovaali [O-vaali]
Pyramid	Pyramidi [PY-ra-mi-di]
Cube	Kuutio [KUU-tio]
Arrow	Nuoli [NUO-li]
Star	Tähti [TAH-ti]
Cylinder	Sylinteri [SY-lin-te-ri]

Write the right words down twice on the next page

Rectangle	....	....
Triangle	....	....
Pyramid	....	....
Arrow	....	....
Star	....	....
Cylinder	....	....
Oval	....	....
Square	....	....
Star	....	....
Cube	....	....
Cirkel	....	....
Pyramid	....	....
Cylinder	....	....
Cirkel	....	....
Square	....	....
Rectangle	....	....
Triangle	....	....
Oval	....	....
Cube	....	....
Arrow	....	....

Week 7

Day 43: House Parts

Roof	Katto [KAT-to]
Door	Ovi [O-vi]
Window	Ikkuna [IK-ku-na]
Floor	Lattia [LAT-ti-a]
Wall	Seinä [SEI-na]
Ceiling	Katto [KAT-to]
Stairs	Portaat [POR-ta-at]
Bathroom	Kylpyhuone [KYLP-y-huo-ne]
Kitchen	Keittiö [KEIT-tio]
Bedroom	Makuuhuone [MA-kuu-huo-ne]

Write the right words down twice on the next page

Wall	....	....
Door	....	....
Stairs	....	....
Ceiling	....	....
Floor	....	....
Wall	....	....
Ceiling	....	....
Bedroom	....	....
Stairs	....	....
Bathroom	....	....
Kitchen	....	....
Bedroom	....	....
Roof	....	....
Door	....	....
Window	....	....
Floor	....	....
Roof	....	....
Bathroom	....	....
Kitchen	....	....
Window	....	....

Week 7

Day 44: Around the House

Plant	Kasvi [KAS-vi]
Watering can	Kastelukannu [KAS-te-lu-kan-nu]
Shed	Lato [LA-to]
Doorbell	Ovikello [O-vi-kel-lo]
Fence	Aita [AI-ta]
Mailbox	Postilaatikko [POS-ti-la-a-tik-ko]
Lawn mower	Ruohonleikkuri [RUO-hon-LEIK-ku-ri]
Wheelbarrow	Kottikärryt [KOT-ti-kar-ryt]
Shovel	Lapio [LA-pio]
Bench	Penkki [PEN-kki]

Write the right words down twice on the next page

Watering can	....	....
Shed	....	....
Doorbell	....	....
Mailbox	....	....
Bench	....	....
Fence	....	....
Wheelbarrow	....	....
Shed	....	....
Mailbox	....	....
Bench	....	....
Lawn mower	....	....
Wheelbarrow	....	....
Shovel	....	....
Plant	....	....
Watering can	....	....
Doorbell	....	....
Fence	....	....
Lawn mower	....	....
Shovel	....	....
Plant	....	....

Week 7

Day 45: Face

Eyes	Silmät [SIL-mat]
Nose	Nenä [NE-na]
Mouth	Suu [SUU]
Ears	Korvat [KOR-vat]
Cheeks	Posket [POS-ket]
Forehead	Otsa [OT-sa]
Chin	Leuka [LEU-ka]
Lips	Huulet [HUU-let]
Teeth	Hampaat [HAM-paat]
Eyebrows	Kulmakarvat [KUL-ma-kar-vat]

Write the right words down twice on the next page

Eyebrows	....	....
Nose	....	....
Chin	....	....
Forehead	....	....
Ears	....	....
Cheeks	....	....
Forehead	....	....
Chin	....	....
Nose	....	....
Lips	....	....
Teeth	....	....
Eyebrows	....	....
Eyes	....	....
Lips	....	....
Teeth	....	....
Mouth	....	....
Ears	....	....
Mouth	....	....
Cheeks	....	....
Eyes	....	....

Week 7

Day 46: Bathroom

Sink	Pesuallas [PE-su-al-las]
Toilet	WC [VEE-SEE]
Shower	Suihku [SUIH-ku]
Bathtub	Kylpyamme [KYLP-y-am-me]
Mirror	Peili [PEI-li]
Towel	Pyyhe [PYY-he]
Soap	Saippua [SAIP-pu-a]
Toothbrush	Hammasharja [HAM-mas-har-ja]
Shampoo	Shampoo [SHAM-poo] (English pronunciation)
Hairdryer	Hiustenkuivaaja [HIUS-ten-KUI-vaa-ja]

Write the right words down twice on the next page

Mirror	....	....
Sink	....	....
Hairdryer	....	....
Shower	....	....
Bathtub	....	....
Mirror	....	....
Towel	....	....
Soap	....	....
Toothbrush	....	....
Toilet	....	....
Shampoo	....	....
Towel	....	....
Soap	....	....
Hairdryer	....	....
Sink	....	....
Toilet	....	....
Shower	....	....
Bathtub	....	....
Toothbrush	....	....
Shampoo	....	....

Week 7

Day 47: Living Room

Sofa	Sohva [SOH-va]
Television	Televisio [te-le-VI-sio]
Coffee table	Sohvapöytä [SOH-va-poy-ta]
Bookshelf	Kirjahylly [KIR-ja-hyl-ly]
Lamp	Lamppu [LAM-ppu]
Rug	Matto [MAT-to]
Cushion	Tyyny [TYYN-y]
Remote control	Kaukosäädin [KAU-ko-SAA-din]
Curtains	Verhot [VER-hot]
Fireplace	Takka [TAK-ka]

Write the right words down twice on the next page

Rug	....	....
Sofa	....	....
Remote control	....	....
Television	....	....
Coffee table	....	....
Bookshelf	....	....
Lamp	....	....
Cushion	....	....
Curtains	....	....
Fireplace	....	....
Sofa	....	....
Television	....	....
Fireplace	....	....
Lamp	....	....
Rug	....	....
Cushion	....	....
Remote control	....	....
Curtains	....	....
Bookshelf	....	....
Coffee table	....	....

Week 7

Day 48: Finance

Budget	Budjetti [BUD-jet-ti]
Savings	Säästöt [SAA-stot]
Debt	Velka [VEL-ka]
Income	Tulo [TU-lo]
Expenses	Menot [ME-not]
Bank account	Pankkitili [PANK-ki-ti-li]
Credit card	Luottokortti [LUOT-to-kort-ti]
Interest	Korko [KOR-ko]
Loan	Laina [LAI-na]
Stock market	Osakemarkkinat [O-sa-ke-MARK-ki-nat]

Write the right words down twice on the next page

Savings	....	....
Loan	....	....
Debt	....	....
Income	....	....
Expenses	....	....
Budget	....	....
Income	....	....
Expenses	....	....
Interest	....	....
Loan	....	....
Stock market	....	....
Budget	....	....
Bank account	....	....
Credit card	....	....
Debt	....	....
Savings	....	....
Interest	....	....
Bank account	....	....
Credit card	....	....
Stock market	....	....

Week 7

Day 49: Books

Writer	Kirjailija [KIR-jail-ija]
Page	Sivu [SI-vu]
Table of Contents	Sisällysluettelo [si-SALLYS-lu-et-te-lo]
Foreword	Johdanto [JOH-dan-to]
Introduction	Esipuhe [E-si-pu-he]
Front cover	Etukansi [E-tu-kan-si]
Back cover	Takakansi [TA-ka-kan-si]
Text	Teksti [TEK-sti]
Title	Otsikko [OT-sik-ko]
Picture	Kuva [KU-va]

Write the right words down twice on the next page

Front cover ....

Table of Contents ....

Title ....

Picture ....

Introduction ....

Back cover ....

Page ....

Foreword ....

Title ....

Text ....

Back cover ....

Picture ....

Writer ....

Page ....

Table of Contents ....

Foreword ....

Introduction ....

Front cover ....

Writer ....

Text ....

Week 8

Day 50: Law

Witness	Tuomioistuin [TUO-mio-IS-tuin]
Justice	Oikeus [OI-keus]
Judge	Tuomari [TUO-ma-ri]
Victim	Uhri [UH-ri]
Perpetrator	Tekijä [TE-ki-ja]
Court	Todistaja [TO-dis-ta-ja]
Evidence	Näyttö [NAYT-to]
Lawyer	Asianajaja [ASIA-na-ja-ja]
Crime	Rikos [RI-kos]
Government	Hallitus [HAL-li-tus]

Write the right words down twice on the next page

Perpetrator	....	....
Court	....	....
Justice	....	....
Evidence	....	....
Victim	....	....
Government	....	....
Judge	....	....
Victim	....	....
Perpetrator	....	....
Court	....	....
Evidence	....	....
Lawyer	....	....
Crime	....	....
Government	....	....
Witness	....	....
Justice	....	....
Crime	....	....
Judge	....	....
Witness	....	....
Lawyer	....	....

More words for you

Questions	Kysymykset	....	....
Answers	Vastaukset	....	....
Think	Ajatella	....	....
Know	Tietää	....	....
Understand	Ymmärtää	....	....
Show	Näyttää	....	....
Feel	Tuntea	....	....
Hear	Kuulla	....	....
Take	Ottaa	....	....
Give	Antaa	....	....
Book	Kirja	....	....
Chair	Tuoli	....	....
Table	Pöytä	....	....
Telephone	Puhelin	....	....
Computer	Tietokone	....	....
Game	Peli	....	....
Mountain	Vuori	....	....
Forest	Metsä	....	....
River	Joki	....	....
City	Kaupunki	....	....
Country	Maa	....	....
Sea	Meri	....	....

Sun	Aurinko	....	....
Moon	Kuu	....	....
Man	Mies	....	....
Woman	Nainen	....	....
Child	Lapsi	....	....
Family	Perhe	....	....
Friend	Ystävä	....	....
House	Talo	....	....
Car	Auto	....	....
Work	Työ	....	....
School	Koulu	....	....
University	Yliopisto	....	....
Eat	Syödä	....	....
Drink	Juoda	....	....
Beer	Olut	....	....
Wine	Viini	....	....
Cheese	Juusto	....	....
Big	Suuri	....	....
Small	Pieni	....	....
Good	Hyvä	....	....
Bad	Huono	....	....
Young	Nuori	....	....
Old	Vanha	....	....

Beautiful	Kaunis	....	....
Ugly	Ruma	....	....
New	Uusi	....	....
Fast	Nopea	....	....
Slow	Hidas	....	....
Warm	Lämmin	....	....
Cold	Kylmä	....	....
Friendly	Ystävällinen	....	....
Unfriendly	Epäystävällinen	....	....
Easy	Helppo	....	....
Heavy	Raskas	....	....
Expensive	Kallis	....	....
Cheap	Halpa	....	....
Quiet	Hiljainen	....	....
Be	Olla	....	....
Have	Omistaa	....	....
Do	Tehdä	....	....
Go	Mennä	....	....
Come	Tulla	....	....
See	Nähdä	....	....
Hear	Kuulla	....	....
Speak	Puhua	....	....
Read	Lukea	....	....

Write	Kirjoittaa	....	....
Eat	Syödä	....	....
Drink	Juoda	....	....
Run	Juosta	....	....
Sleep	Nukkua	....	....
Work	Työskennellä	....	....
Learn	Oppia	....	....
Help	Auta	....	....
Play	Pelata	....	....
Search	Etsiä	....	....
Buy	Ostaa	....	....
Stay	Pysyä	....	....
Stand	Seisoa	....	....
Sit	Istua	....	....
Carry	Kantaa	....	....
Meet	Tavata	....	....
Leave	Lähteä	....	....
Begin	Aloittaa	....	....
Tell	Kertoa	....	....
Win	Voittaa	....	....
Lose	Hävitä	....	....
Open	Avata	....	....
Close	Sulkea	....	....

Improve	Parantaa	....	....
Explain	Selittää	....	....
Follow	Seurata	....	....
Remember	Muistaa	....	....
Forget	Unohtaa	....	....
Pay	Maksaa	....	....
Sell	Myydä	....	....
Send	Lähettää	....	....
Receive	Vastaanottaa	....	....
Decide	Päättää	....	....
Visit	Vierailla	....	....
Love	Rakastaa	....	....
Hate	Vihaa	....	....
Celebrate	Juhlia	....	....
Dance	Tanssia	....	....
Sing	Laulaa	....	....
Jump	Hypätä	....	....
Newspaper	Sanomalehti	....	....
Magazine	Aikakauslehti	....	....
Letter	Kirje	....	....
Card	Kortti	....	....
Gift	Lahja	....	....
Party	Juhla	....	....

Holidays	Lomat	....	....
Travel	Matkustaa	....	....
Photo	Valokuva	....	....
Camera	Kamera	....	....
Light	Valo	....	....
Art	Taide	....	....
Culture	Kulttuuri	....	....
History	Historia	....	....
Nature	Luonto	....	....
Environment	Ympäristö	....	....
Weather	Sää	....	....
Rain	Sade	....	....
Snow	Lumi	....	....
Ice	Jää	....	....
Fast	Nopea	....	....
Slow	Hidas	....	....
Early	Aikainen	....	....
Late	Myöhäinen	....	....
Simple	Yksinkertainen	....	....
Difficult	Vaikea	....	....
Strong	Vahva	....	....
Weak	Heikko	....	....
Correct	Oikein	....	....

English	Finnish		
Wrong	Väärin		
Safe	Turvallinen		
Dangerous	Vaarallinen		
Important	Tärkeä		
Interesting	Mielenkiintoinen		
Boring	Tylsä		
Happy	Onnellinen		
Sad	Surullinen		
Healthy	Terve		
Sick	Sairas		
Tired	Väsynyt		
Animal	Eläin		
Dog	Koira		
Cat	Kissa		
Bird	Lintu		
Fish	Kala		
Horse	Hevonen		
Street	Katu		
Way	Tie		
Bridge	Silta		
Square	Aukio		

Help Us Share Your Thoughts!

Dear reader,

We hope you enjoyed reading this book as much as we enjoyed making it for you. This book is part of a special collection from **Skriuwer (www.skriuwer.com)**, a global community dedicated to creating books that make language learning an engaging and enjoyable experience.

Our journey doesn't end here. We believe that every reader is part of our growing family. If there was anything in this book you did not like, or if you have suggestions for improvement, we are all ears! Do not hesitate to contact us at **kontakt@skriuwer.com**. Your feedback is extremely valuable in making our books even better.

If you enjoyed your experience, we would be thrilled to hear about it! Consider leaving a review on the website where you purchased this book. Your positive reviews not only warm our hearts, but also help other language learners to discover and enjoy our books.

Thank you very much for choosing **Skriuwer**. Let's continue to explore the wonders of languages and the joy of learning together.

Warm regards,
The Skriuwer Team

Printed in Great Britain
by Amazon

48812482R00064